BOOTS, BUCKLES, & BOLOS

JIM ARNDT

Gibbs Smith

First Edition
29 28 27 26 25 5 4 3 2 1

Published by
Gibbs Smith
570 N. Sportsplex Drive
Kaysville, Utah 84037
1.800.835.4993 orders
www.gibbs-smith.com

Designed by Sheryl Dickert
Printed and bound in China

Library of Congress Control Number: 202495160
ISBN: 978-1-4236-6904-3

This product is made of FSC®-certified and other controlled material.

Publisher's note: What is traditionally called an "Indian head" buckle or bolo is an item of Western-style jewelry that features an image of a Native American leader, or chief, often wearing a headdress. For purposes of this publication, we use the names that are traditionally used by jewelry craftspeople or designers.

To Nathalie

Iconic Western Symbols

Each of us has images in our minds and, often, special memories that remind us of the American West landscapes: mountains and their streams, deserts and wide-open spaces, breathtaking sunsets, bison roaming prairies and plains. On a more notable level, the freedom of the Old West, the wildness of bar brawls, bank robberies, and shoot-outs join our collected memories of a time and place.

Central among these visions is "The Cowboy," on horseback, independent, riding over a hill or across a stream, rounding up cattle, or pursuing horse thieves. The cowboy is a true American icon.

What defines him? In addition to his lifestyle, the attire of the American cowboy in his daily work has become iconic. Particularly, boots, buckles, and bolo ties have been adopted and upscaled in high fashion and for everyday wear.

Cowgirls, cowboys, or anyone who loves Western wear can put on these iconic symbols of the cowboy, wherever we are in the world. They are always associated with the American West and dreams of how to be a cowboy.

BOOTS

Many origin stories exist, and the evolution of the boot to cowboy boots takes one on a historic journey through centuries. In earlier times, boots were of plain design, functional and able to withstand the ruggedness of a cowboy's work, keeping him mostly dry during wet times and helping to protect his feet from the stomping of horses and cattle, and giving his ankles and calves some measure of protection against prickly sagebrush and weeds.

Vintage boots still intrigue collectors and continue to be highly sought after. However, as time went on, and boot makers continued to perfect their craft, designs became fancier, more playful, and personal to the customer. What had once been basic evolved into handsome, beautiful, decorative, and multicolored footwear.

Today, there are styles for everyone, and many pairs of boots are works of art, with images of western icons from skulls to flowers to personal imagery. From the hands of talented boot craftspeople, future designs are limited only by one's imagination!

ABOVE: Vintage Kids' red-top boots.

OPPOSITE: T-Rex, a Christmas gift for his grandson, by master boot maker John Weinkauf.

ABOVE: Well-worn inlaid horse heads, courtesy Justin and Tara Kent.

OPPOSITE: Beloved and muddy kids' buckin' broncs.

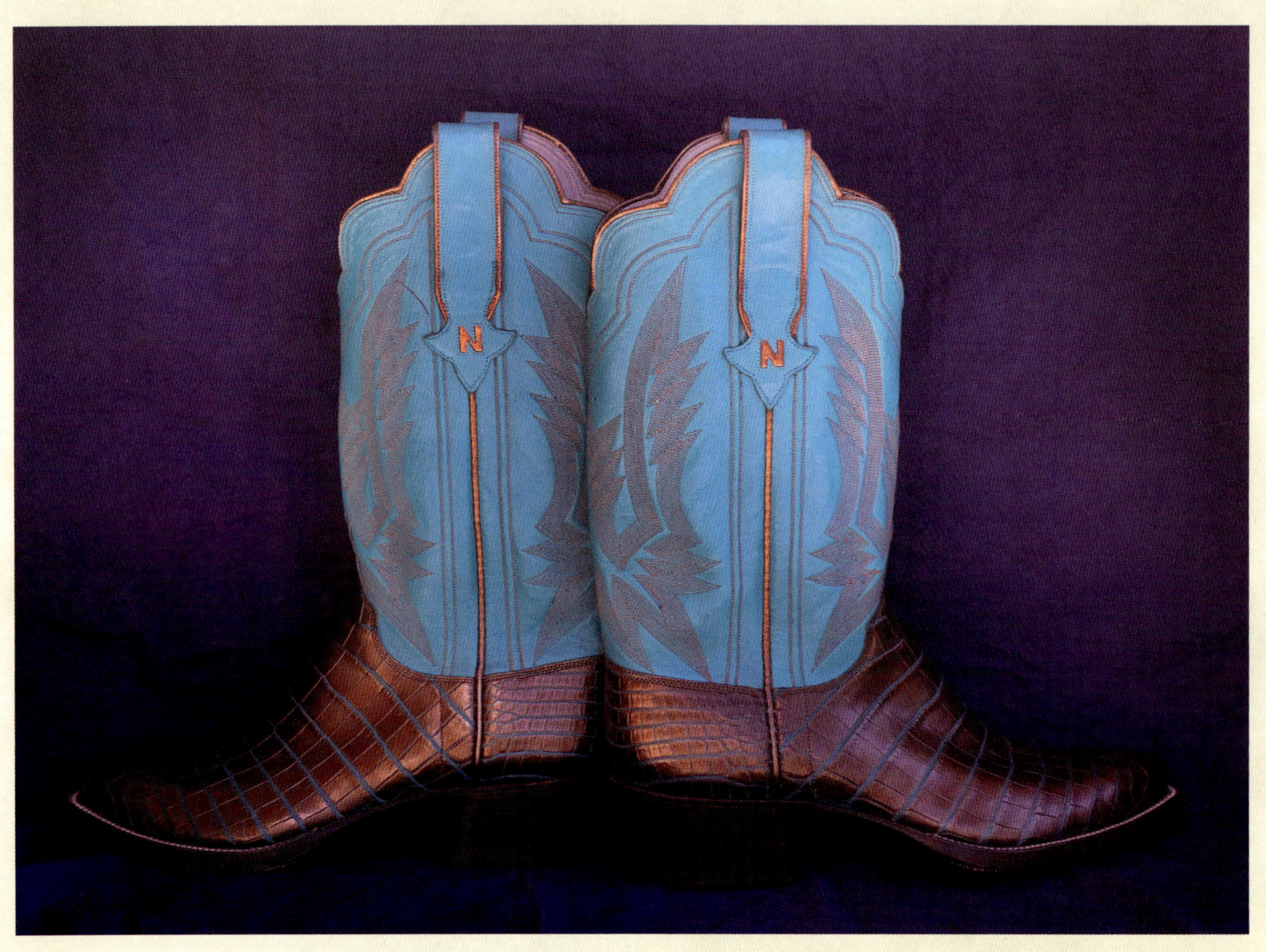

ABOVE: Turquoise-and-copper gator "N" monograms; designed by Nathalie Kent; made by M. L. Leddy.

OPPOSITE: Shiny and sparkly Stetson kids' boots.

ABOVE: Butterflies are always a popular motif.

OPPOSITE: Red-top, classic inlay butterfly.

OPPOSITE AND ABOVE: Classic butterfly boots in two shades of green.

OPPOSITE: Starburst tops with chopped square toes.

LEFT: Famous Tres Outlaws cross boots with rhinestones on silver, inlaid in copper leather.

N
K

Eiffel Towers for my French cowgirl.

OPPOSITE AND RIGHT: Elaborate inlay and overlay work; designed by Nathalie Kent; made by Dave Little.

CENTER: Mule ears with rhinestones, by Rocketbuster.

OPPOSITE: Armand Ventillo Couture special collection, Paris, France.

ABOVE: Longhorn propellers and flowers on amazingly detailed wingtips, by Dave Little.

ABOVE: Over-the-top skull boots, by Tres Outlaws.

OPPOSITE: Cutouts and filigree, outlined on the foot with tiny, fluted, sterling silver conchos, by Tres Outlaws.

ABOVE LEFT: Vintage eagle boots; courtesy Mike Cavender.

ABOVE RIGHT: Vintage eagle boots with mule ears and silver toes; courtesy Mike Cavender.

OPPOSITE: Inlaid eagles, by Dave Little.

Classic 1960s stovetop style with flaming wingtips and foxing; by Little's Boot Company; courtesy Mike Cavender.

Eagle inlays on vintage red leather.

TOP AND BOTTOM: It's all about the heels. Great for dancing, walking, or gawking.

Spectacular wing pattern; courtesy Mike Cavender.

OPPOSITE: Love and luck in tall, well-heeled hearts and horseshoes; vintage.

ABOVE: Olson-Stelzer classics with hearts and a scalloped top edge.

OPPOSITE: Exquisitely tooled, with Virgin Mary inset, by Cock of the Walk Boots.

LEFT: Rare "Forty Roses of Guadalupe" tooled and painted boots, by Tres Outlaws; courtesy Nathalie Kent.

OPPOSITE TOP LEFT: Mule-eared, piteado-inspired, inlaid "N" boots.

OPPOSITE BOTTOM LEFT: Bucking horse boots, by Hyer; courtesy Mike Cavender.

OPPOSITE RIGHT: Tall "Harpo Hearts," by Stallion.

LEFT: Full piteado-embroidered cactus boots, by Liberty.

Special Cavender "Mike" boots.

OPPOSITE: Unique stitch pattern on foot and uppers.

ABOVE: Judy Lynn's boots, 1960s. Nudie at his best!

OPPOSITE: Art Miller's 1960s copper and rhinestone boots, by Nudie.

OPPOSITE: Nathalie's pride: Stars and Stripes America boots, by Back at the Ranch.

ABOVE LEFT: Texas flag with cactus, by Dave Little.

ABOVE RIGHT: U.S. flag boots, by Dave Little.

ABOVE: Boots of Major Lynn White (1838–1915), at one time the world's smallest man (23 inches tall) and a performer in the W. A. Gibbs Carnival; courtesy Mike Cavender.

OPPOSITE: Best of the best: full alligator, fully silver laced boots, by Dave Little.

LEFT: Vintage stovetop boots, stitched overall; courtesy Mike Cavender.

CENTER: Early rodeo cowgirl boots with attitude; courtesy Roxanne Thurman.

RIGHT: Squash blossom inlays, by Las Cruces Boot Company; courtesy Gene Autry Western Heritage Museum.

ABOVE: "Celeste Stars," overall stitched, by Old Gringo for Nathalie.

OPPOSITE: Stitched turquoise on chocolate leather, by Old Gringo.

OPPOSITE: Incredible tooling and lacing on the late Tyler Beard's personal longhorns and stars boot. Made by Back at the Ranch; tooling by Bob Dellis; courtesy Mike Cavender.

ABOVE LEFT: The author's well-worn boots.

ABOVE RIGHT: Classy black-and-brown inlays with fancy wingtips and foxing.

OPPOSITE: Vintage tooled buckin' broncs.

ABOVE: "Tarita" red boots with one-piece regal tops with sterling silver-domed stars by Doug Magnus; made by Stallion.

"Taos" inlaid, overlaid, and laced boots, by Back at the Ranch.

LEFT: Pink flaming heart "Love and Peace" boots, by Liberty.

RIGHT: "Monet" pink-and-white cutouts, by Back at the Ranch.

"Gypsy Rose" inlaid and overlaid flower boots, by Back at the Ranch.

"Monet" in blue and white, by Back at the Ranch.

OPPOSITE: "El Rancho" family, by Back at the Ranch.

LEFT: Stitched "Peacock," by Back at the Ranch.

OPPOSITE: "O' Susanna," inlaid and overlaid flowers, by Back at the Ranch.

LEFT: "Dia de los Muertos," tooled and hand painted, by Back at the Ranch.

OPPOSITE: Classic perforated wingtips and flowered tops, vintage, by Justin Boots.

ABOVE LEFT: Vintage longhorns.

BELOW LEFT: Vintage classic flowers.

BUCKLES

Every rodeo cowboy has a buckle. Today, most are won at local rodeos, but the very tough, talented, skilled, and lucky cowboys might walk away with a trophy buckle won at a major national event.

The best silversmiths and engravers create unbelievable works of art. In addition to trophy buckles, silversmiths work with many a fashion cowgirl or cowboy to produce belt jewelry that is personalized or monogrammed. A collector seeking a custom buckle can work with the silversmith to come up with a design that suits their taste, such as a Texas longhorn, an American flag, a skull, a chief headdress, a brand, or a beautiful design with inlay work. You will see that the design possibilities are exciting and endless as you look through these outstanding examples.

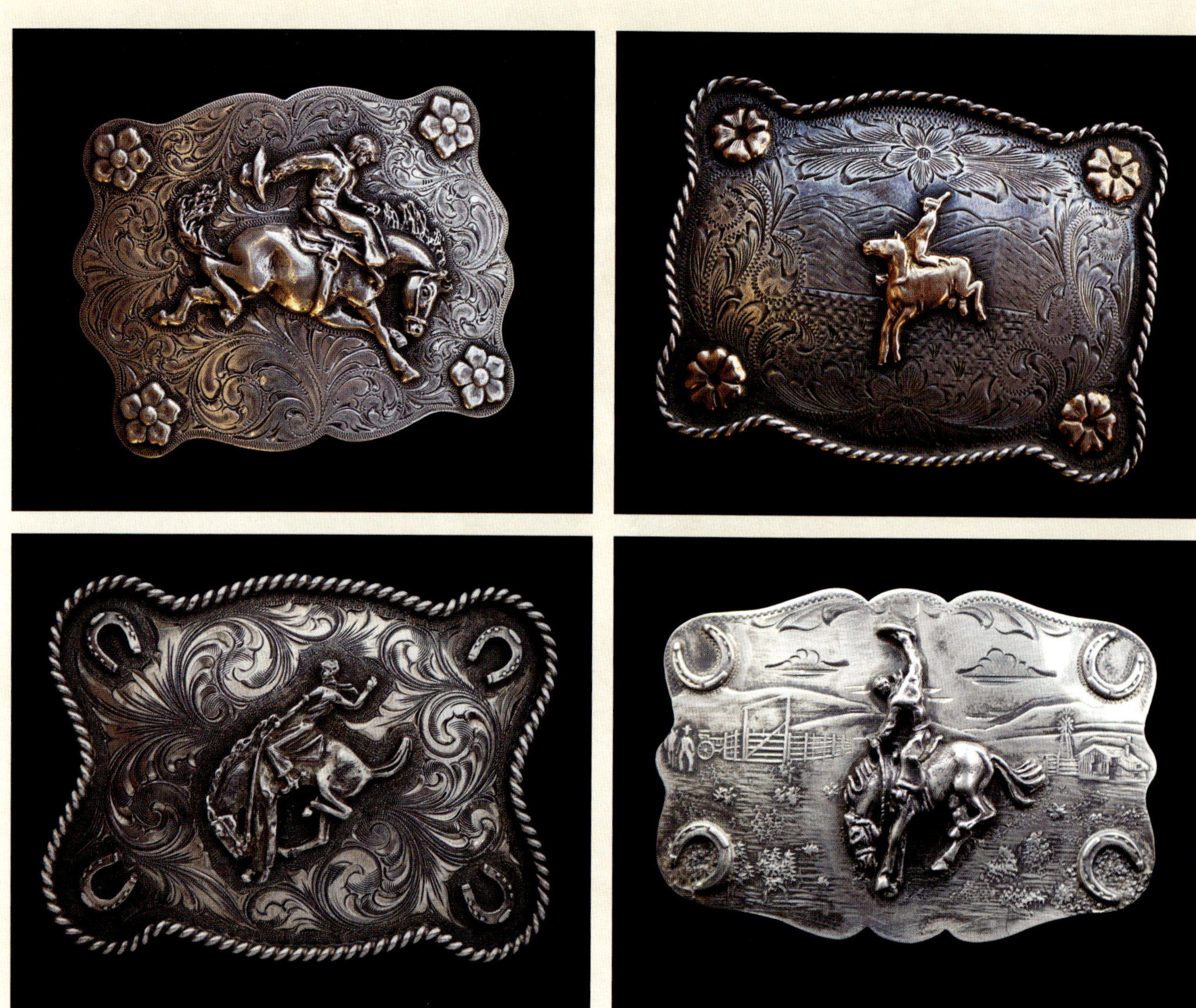

PAGE 64: Classic vintage cowboy buckle; Ralph Tingle Collection.

Buckin' Broncs in sterling.
CLOCKWISE ABOVE, FROM TOP LEFT: Ronnie Dunn's stage buckle, by Bohlin; vintage; by Comstock; by Clint Orms Engravers & Silversmiths.

Vintage Comstock pony rider.

FLYING "A" RANCH
1950

OPPOSITE: Flying "A" Ranch buckin' bronc, by Comstock.

LEFT: Two old Chinle Champion buckles, hand engraved.

Sterling silver *Horse Whisperer* buckle, originally designed for Tom Booker (played by Robert Redford in the movie), by Edward H. Bohlin Company.

Styles and sizes for different tastes.
Makers, CLOCKWISE ABOVE, FROM UPPER LEFT: Clint Mortenson, Comstock, Bohlin, Clint Orms.

Variations on the flying "A" logo.

OPPOSITE TOP: Bohlin longhorn.

OPPOSITE BOTTOM: Clint Orms three-color gold.

LEFT TOP: Hopi overlay.

LEFT BOTTOM: Gene Autry buckle, by Bohlin.

FLYING A RANCH
1950

OPPOSITE TOP: Flying "A" Ranch 1950, by Clint Mortenson.

OPPOSITE BOTTOM: JA brand buckle, by Clint Mortenson.

LEFT TOP: Canyon de Chelly, by Clint Mortenson.

LEFT BOTTOM: Cutout "A" star set in silver and overlay gold, by Holland's.

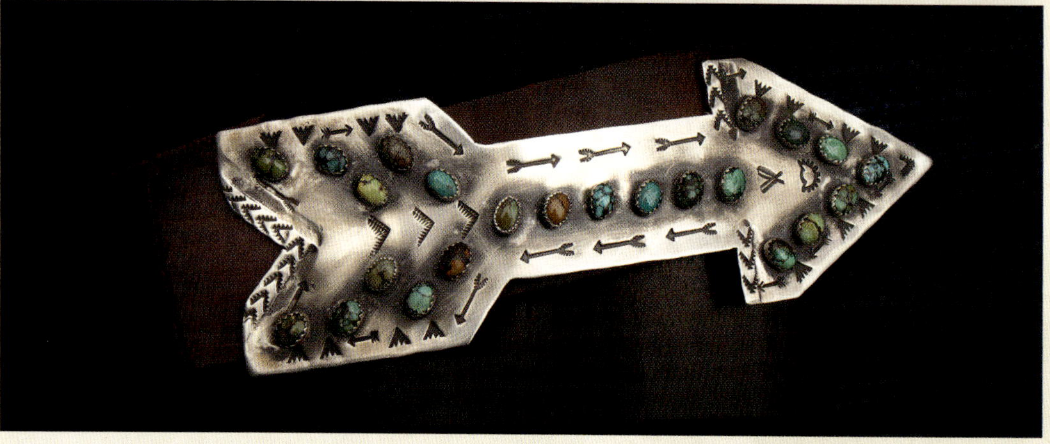

OPPOSITE TOP: Nathalie-designed cross and arrows, by Clint Orms Engravers & Silversmiths.

OPPOSITE BOTTOM: Extra-large sterling arrow with turquoise cabochons, by Adrienne Teeguarden.

ABOVE: Arrows and rubies in a gold cross; designed by Nathalie Kent, made by Clint Orms.

OPPOSITE: Sterling heart with overlaid crossed arrows; designed by Nathalie Kent, made by Clint Orms.

TOP LEFT AND RIGHT: Two Clint Orms buckles, designed by Nathalie.

BOTTOM: Hand-engraved silver ranger buckle set with accents in gold, by Matt Hackett.

ABOVE: Longhorn and good-luck horseshoe, by Clint Mortenson.

OPPOSITE: Longhorns collection. CLOCKWISE FROM TOP LEFT: With stars, by Comstock; with gold horns, by Clint Orms; longhorn, by Clint Orms; tribal style, by Comstock.

ABOVE: Deep-engraved sterling star and arrows, by Clint Orms.

OPPOSITE TOP: Sterling ranger-style buckle set, by John Rippel.

OPPOSITE BOTTOM: Triple horsehead with silver coins.

ABOVE: Collection of Nathalie's trophy buckles, CLOCKWISE FROM TOP LEFT: Vintage; Roger Skeet Sr.; vintage; Jerry Faires.

OPPOSITE: Two thunderbirds, by Al Somers.

Clyde

OPPOSITE TOP: Clyde, "the most famous movie star buffalo," by Clint Mortenson.

OPPOSITE BOTTOM: Sterling silver buffalo and arrows, by Chet Vogt.

LEFT: Three ranger buckle sets: Buffalo Bill, Spur, and Lariat, all by Clint Mortenson.

ROCKIN' JH RANCH
1943

OPPOSITE: Gold and silver Rockin' JH Ranch, a commemorative buckle for French music artist and actor Johnny Hallyday (1943–2017), by Clint Mortenson.

TOP LEFT: Money buckle, by Clint Mortenson.

BOTTOM LEFT: American flag, by Clint Orms.

BUFFALO
BILLS
WILD
WEST
PARIS
19
95
Clint Mortenson

OPPOSITE: Buffalo Bill's Wild West, Paris, by Clint Mortenson.

TOP LEFT: *Magnificent Seven* stuntmen's buckle, by Clint Mortenson.

BOTTOM LEFT: Vintage brass Tom Mix pistol buckle.

ABOVE: Sterling silver cutout and stamped Native American buckle, by Al Somers.

OPPOSITE TOP: Fully studded belt with sterling silver, open-center buckle, by Jack Walker.

OPPOSITE BOTTOM LEFT: Classic Native American–style concho made into a buckle.

OPPOSITE BOTTOM RIGHT: Raised-engraved overlay and flowers, by Clint Orms.

OPPOSITE TOP: Vintage Mexican piteado with matching horseshoe buckles.

OPPOSITE BOTTOM LEFT: Horseshoe ranger set, by Edward H. Bohlin.

OPPOSITE BOTTOM RIGHT: Fleur de lys buckle, by Adrienne Teeguarden.

TOP LEFT: Overlaid and engraved four-piece ranger set, by Matt Hackett.

BOTTOM LEFT: Four-piece Longhorn, boots, and pistols in sterling and gold, by Chet Vogt.

Incredible hand-beaded portrait buckles by Marcus Amerman; courtesy Nathalie.

ABOVE: Jackson Sundown, a mythic Nez Perce bronco-bustin' rodeo rider who won a Saddle Bronc Champion at Pendleton in the early 1900s.

OPPOSITE TOP: Crazy Horse, Lakota leader of the Oglala.

OPPOSITE BOTTOM: Little Chief, a Northern Cheyenne warrior.

ABOVE: Ronnie Dunn buckle, by Sweet Bird Studio.

OPPOSITE TOP: Custom brass and sterling eagle buckle, by Lakota Visions.

OPPOSITE BOTTOM: Contemporary three-piece ranger set with eagle and feathers, by Brenda Rimer Romero.

TOP: Bohlin Indian head with chief's headdress. It was a bookend before it became a buckle; courtesy Nathalie Kent.

BOTTOM: Oval Indian head with chief's headdress and scrolling, by Bohlin.

TOP: Classic Indian head in gold and silver, with a rope edge, by Bohlin.

BOTTOM: Profile Indian head with peace pipe, by Clint Orms.

Indian head with gold tipis, by Matt Hackett.

TOP: Three-piece gold overlay Indian heads, arrows, and tipis, by Sunset Trails.

BOTTOM: Three-piece Indian head with bow and arrows, by Chet Vogt.

TOP: An Adrienne Teeguarden cross on cross with turquoise.

BOTTOM: Extra-large, 1970s, open-center sterling buckle; Nathalie Collection.

Navajo open-center buckle, antique; Nathalie Collection.

Turquoise and jet cross, by Lee Downey.

CLOCKWISE FROM TOP LEFT: Al Somers, maker; Jerry Faires, maker; Navajo trophy style; 1940s Navajo.

OPPOSITE: A 1940s concho with turquoise and a unique boot keeper.

TOP: Antique concho with turquoise.

BOTTOM: Very rare tufa-cast buckle with turquoise cabochons; Nathalie Collection.

OPPOSITE: Spectacular, raised-engraved, Carico Lake turquoise and jet trophy buckle, by Lee Downey.

TOP: "Duce Ferro Comitante" skulls and sword buckle, by Richard Stump.

BOTTOM: Inlay in sterling silver, by Albert Platero; courtesy John Rippel.

OPPOSITE: Mokume-gane technique skull with turquoise, by Lee Downey.

TOP: The "Johnny Bones" martini, pistol, and dice buckle, by Nick Cunningham for Vogt.

BOTTOM: Bone skull in sterling, by Lee Downey.

Vintage 1940s concho belt.

TOP: Concho belt, by Adrienne Teeguarden.

BOTTOM: Concho belt, by Geraldine Yazzie, Navajo.

ABOVE: Zuni concho belt, 1940s; Branson Collection, courtesy Nathalie Kent.

OPPOSITE LEFT: Vintage concho belt with butterflies.

OPPOSITE CENTER: Amazing turquoise cabochons, by Kenny Bracken.

OPPOSITE RIGHT: Arnold Goldstein rectangular conchos.

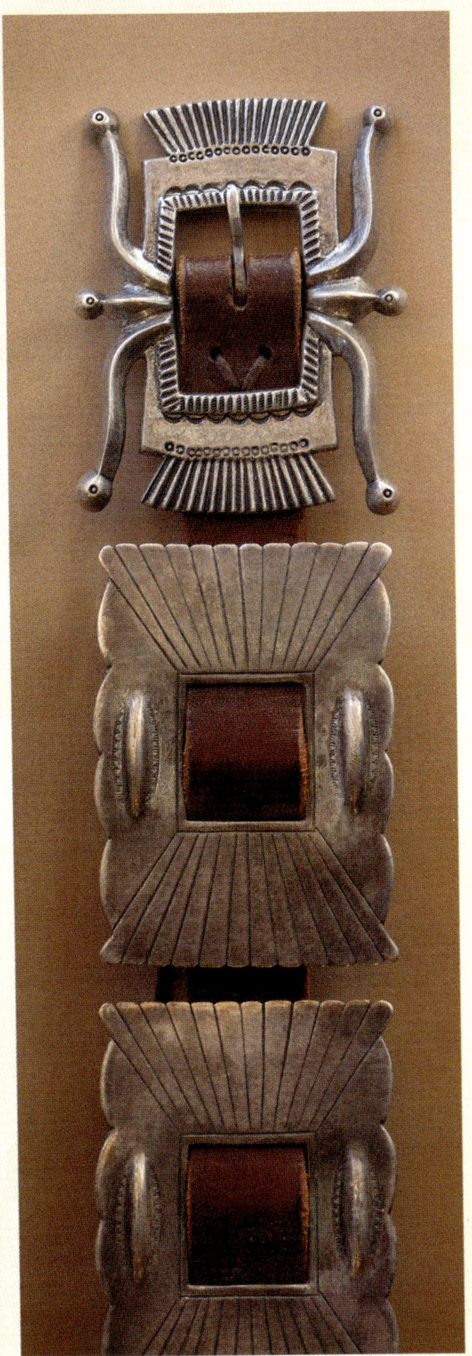

BOLOS

Traditional western bolo ties are a braided leather cord, usually with a metal slide and often with metal tips on the ends of the cord. The bolo tie is recognized as the tie of the Southwest and is the official tie of New Mexico, Arizona, and Texas.

Stylistically, bolos can be made of many different materials, chiefly metals and multi-stone inlays, but silver and turquoise have been predominant. Bolo designs vary from eagles, thunderbirds, lizards, and bear paws to buffalo heads, cowboy hats, Native American headdresses, rodeo emblems, crosses, and western stars. It all adds panache and pizazz to the wearer's outfits. The bolo tie is a true Western fashion accessory.

PAGE 118: Deep-stamped sterling cross, by Adrienne Teeguarden.

OPPOSITE: Sterling longhorn, by Arnold Goldstein.

ABOVE LEFT: "Cowboy Life" in copper, with fun boot tips.

ABOVE RIGHT: Vintage cowboys, by silversmith Roger Miller.

OPPOSITE: Two vintage classic Southwest Kachinas in sterling and turquoise.

LEFT: Tall hoop dancer in sterling and turquoise.

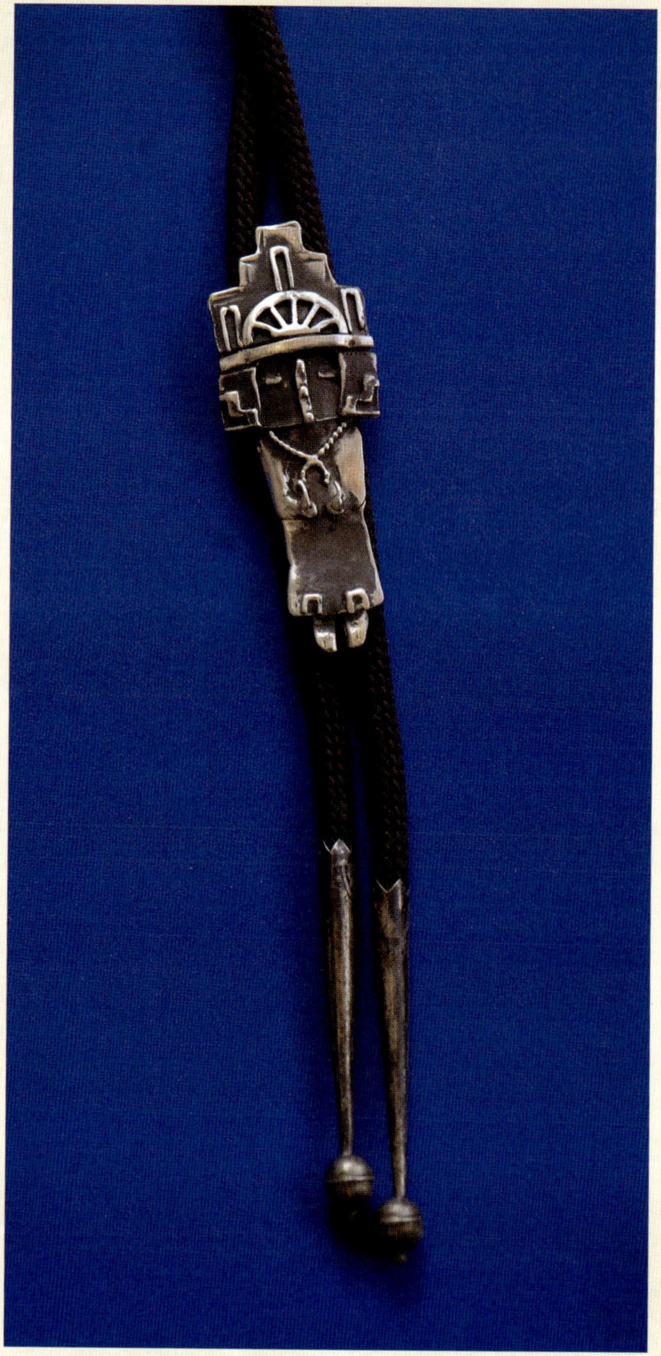

OPPOSITE TOP LEFT: Zuni silver and multi-stone inlay, 1950s. Courtesy Morningstar.

OPPOSITE BOTTOM LEFT: Zuni inlay headdress; courtesy Wahoo!

OPPOSITE RIGHT: Hemis Kachina by Catherine Maziere.

LEFT: Apache dancer in a patchwork of mixed inlaid stones, by a Zuni artist.

OPPOSITE LEFT: Rocker-engraved peyote bird, by Robert Blanchet.

OPPOSITE RIGHT: Starry horse and bison, by Richard Lindsay; courtesy Amado and JB Pena.

TOP LEFT: Santa Domingo inlay on vinyl, by artist Robert Rosetta.

TOP RIGHT: Classic Santa Domingo overlay on vinyl, by artist Robert Rosetta.

BOTTOM: Mosaic inlaid eagle, by Mary Frances Begaye.

ABOVE LEFT AND RIGHT: Carved and sculpted sterling silver and natural stones, Corn Maiden and Blanket Man, by Buddy Lee.

OPPOSITE: Turquoise mission church, by Buddy Lee.

OPPOSITE TOP LEFT: Horse in silver.

OPPOSITE BOTTOM LEFT: Rearing stallion on boot in sterling, by Mona Van Riper.

OPPOSITE RIGHT: Old engraved boot with turquoise on a horsehair tie.

LEFT: Horse inlay with inlay saddle tips, by J. Mahkee, Zuni; courtesy Gilbert Hampton.

RIGHT: Unique horseshoe with Indian head and turquoise cabochons, by Chet Vogt.

OPPOSITE LEFT: Three-color gold Indian head on sterling, by Sunset Trails.

OPPOSITE RIGHT: Classic three-color gold chief head and tips, by Bohlin.

LEFT: Turquoise in a shadow box.

RIGHT: Antique embossed slide with oval turquoise; Nathalie Collection.

OPPOSITE: Bolo tie for Robert Delannoy in sterling, with turquoise cabochons; Nathalie Kent and Adrienne Teeguarden silversmithing collaboration.

OPPOSITE TOP LEFT: Zia symbol, by John Rippel.

OPPOSITE BOTTOM LEFT: Railroad track-style in sterling, by J. Begay.

OPPOSITE RIGHT: Gold skull casket, by Richard Stump.

LEFT: "Day of the Dead," by Kit Carson.

RIGHT: Stars and stars bolo.

OPPOSITE LEFT: Nathalie store logo, cross with friendship arrows.

OPPOSITE RIGHT: Tipi with turquoise, by Adrienne Teeguarden.

LEFT: Braided and hitched horsehair four-tassel bolo, by Jose Hernandez; designed by Nathalie Kent.

RIGHT: Braided kangaroo laced bolo tie, with pineapple knots.

LEFT: Flying "A" with stars.

RIGHT: Santa Fe Deputy bolo.

OPPOSITE: Rectangular concho on leather, by Love Tokens.

ABOVE LEFT AND RIGHT: Zuni inlaid eagle and inlaid Zuni rainbow dancer; courtesy Rainbow Man.

OVERLEAF: Flying "A" boots, by Little's Boot Company.

Acknowledgments

Thanks to all the talented artists, past and present.

A big thank-you to Madge Baird, editor extraordinaire, for her faithfulness and hard work, and to Sheryl Dickert for her design talent. A huge thank-you and love to Kathy Graves, wordsmith, for helping her little brother.

To all the boot makers, buckle and bolo artists, and collectors, and everyone who contributed, thank you:
Nathalie Kent, Tyler Beard, Evan Voyles, Mike Cavender, Dave Little, Sharon Little, Duane Little, Clint Mortenson, Wendy Lane Henry, Alan Wilkinson, John Weinkauf, Richard Stump, M. L. Leddy, Martha and Wilson Franklin, Roxanne Thurman, Ronnie Dunn, Johnny Hallyday, Marilyn Lennox, Richard Stump, Catherine Mazierre, Mona Van Riper, John Rippel, Marianne and Bob Kapoun, Doug Magnus, Adrianne Teeguarden, Kit Carson, Robert Blanchet, Jerry Faires, James Stegman, Tom Taylor, John Valdes, Everet Apodaca, Les Ochs, Andrew Munana, Michael Mares, Mary Frances Begaye, Marcus Ammerman, Robert Rosetta, Gilbert Hampton, Jay Ann Martin, Mitch Henfrey, Ralph Tingle, JB and Amado Pena, Linda Boles Morgan, Debra and Jock Favour, Jack Pressler, Diane Zamost, and Henry Monahan, Wahoo!, and Morningstar.

As always, most of all, an enormous thank-you to my partner, my friend, my western inspiration, my girl, my love–Nathalie, always in her cowgirl boots and Western wear–for all her love and support.

The Author

Jim Arndt is a nationally recognized advertising and editorial photographer based in Santa Fe, New Mexico. His work has been exhibited in galleries in Minneapolis, Santa Fe, Taos, Austin, and Paris, France. His work is in the permanent photo collection of the History Museum of New Mexico. His clients include Wrangler, Ronnie Dunn, Dodge/Ram, Winchester, Marty Stuart, Harley-Davidson, Marlboro, and Chevrolet. In addition, Jim has taught at the Santa Fe Photographic Workshops.

Arndt's publications include *The Cowboy Boot Book, 100 Years of Western Wear, Art of the Boot, Cowboy Boots, Art of the Cross, Art of the Buckle, Art of the Skull, Art of Turquoise, How to be a Cowboy*, and *Buckaroo Boots*.